Encyclopedia of Places

Contents

Beach	4
Desert	6
Forest	8
Mountain	10
Pond	12
Tundra	14
Index	16

The world has many places.
Find out about some of them in this book.

Beach

All beaches have shores.

Things Found at Some Beaches

Desert

All deserts are dry.

Things Found in Some Deserts

Forest

All forests have trees.

Things Found in Some Forests

pine cone

beetle

ferns

woodpecker

mushrooms

squirrel

9

Mountain

All mountains are tall.

Things Found on Some Mountains

snow

goat

eagle

plant

bear

mountain peak

Pond

All ponds have water.

Things Found in Some Ponds

Tundra

All tundra are cold.

Things Found on Some Tundra

Index

beach	4–5
desert	6–7
forest	8–9
mountain	10–11
pond	12–13
shores	4
trees	8
tundra	14–15
water	12